go! CHINESE 听说读打写

Go 400

Workbook
(Simplified Character Edition)

罗秋昭
Julie LO

薛意梅
Emily YIH

CENGAGE
Learning™

Australia • Brazil • Japan • Korea • Mexico • Singapore • Spain • United Kingdom • United States

Go! Chinese Go400 Workbook
(Simplified Character Edition)
Julie Lo, Emily Yih

Publishing Director / CLT Product Director:
Paul Tan

Product Manager (Outside Asia):
Mei Yun Loh

Product Manager (Asia):
Joyce Tan

Senior Development Editor:
Lan Zhao

Associate Development Editor:
Coco Koh

Editor:
Titus Teo

Senior Graphic Designer:
Melvin Chong

Assistant Publishing Manager:
Pauline Lim

Country Manager (China):
Caroline Ma

Account Manager (China):
Arthur Sun

CLT Coordinator (China):
Mana Wu

Assistant Editor, ELT:
Yuan Ting Soh

ISBN-13: 978-981-4246-49-1
ISBN-10: 981-4246-49-2

Cengage Learning Asia Pte Ltd
5 Shenton Way #01-01
UIC Building
Singapore 068808

Cengage Learning is a leading provider of customized learning solutions with office locations around the globe, including Singapore, the United Kingdom, Australia, Mexico, Brazil, and Japan. Locate your local office at:
www.cengage.com/global

Cengage Learning products are represented in Canada by Nelson Education, Ltd.

For product information, visit **www.cengagesasia.com**

Photo credits
Cover: © Charly Franklin/Taxi/Getty Images ; p.76: 92984050, 92769679 @ 2010 Jupiterimages Corporation.

Printed in Singapore
1 2 3 4 5 14 13 12 11 10

Preface

Go! Chinese, together with *IQChinese Go* multimedia CD-ROM, is a fully integrated Chinese language program that offers an easy, enjoyable, and effective learning experience for learners of Chinese as a foreign language.

The Workbook is an essential component of the *Go! Chinese* series. The exercises are closely linked to the content of each lesson, allowing students to solidify their understanding of and review the lesson learned in the classroom.

The Workbook features the following types of exercises:

- **Foundation Building Exercises**

  Phonetics (*pinyin*), Chinese radicals, vocabulary review, sentence re-ordering, and translation are examples of foundation building exercises. These exercises help students systematically build a solid foundation in the Chinese language.

- **Problem-Solving Exercises**

  Exercises such as crossword puzzles, composing short conversations, and answering questions involving the interpretation of graphs or pictures, provide students with interesting and challenging opportunities to learn the Chinese language through problem-solving tasks.

- **Chinese Typing Exercises**

  The unique characteristic of this series is the use of Chinese typing as an instructional strategy to improve word recognition, listening, and pronunciation skills. The typing activity can be found in the CD-ROM. Students are asked to type characters or sentences as they are read aloud or displayed on the computer screen. They will be alerted if they make a mistake and will be given the chance to correct them. If they do not get it right on the third try, the software provides immediate feedback on how to correct the error. This interactive trial-and-error process allows students to develop self-confidence and learn by doing. Students can use the chart in the Workbook to record their best timings for these typing activities (Sentence Quiz). Students can also keep a separate list of words that they frequently have trouble with for future review.

  The Sentence Quiz exercise comprises four levels.

  ➤ Level 1 – Warm-up Quiz (Look, Listen, and Type): Chinese text, *pinyin*, and audio prompts are provided.

  ➤ Level 2 – Visual-aid Quiz: Only Chinese text is provided. There are no *pinyin* or audio prompts.

  ➤ Level 3 – Audio-aid Quiz: Only audio prompts are provided.

  ➤ Level 4 – Character-selection Quiz: Only Chinese text is provided. After entering the correct *pinyin*, students are required to select the correct character from a list of similar looking characters.

Besides the Sentence Quiz exercises, students can practice Chinese typing in the "Teacher's Assignment" section of the CD-ROM. In these exercises, teachers can vary the level of difficulty based on the students' proficiency level. However, students can only type in numerals and Chinese characters they have learned before. For example, in level Go400, students can only type in Chinese characters* that they have learned in levels Go100 to Go400. Upon completion, the exercises are printable, and there is a time-recording feature to indicate the completion time of each activity. A number of exercises in the Workbook may be completed in the "Teacher's Assignment" section.

* Core vocabulary only; does not include supplementary vocabulary taught in the Textbook.

• Word Recognition and Character Writing Exercises

To help students learn to read and recognize actual Chinese characters, *pinyin* is generally not annotated in the Workbook, except for certain *pinyin*, writing, and vocabulary exercises.

The Workbook also provides Chinese character writing worksheets for a subset of the vocabulary to help students understand and appreciate the characteristics and formation of Chinese characters. Writing can help students remember the Chinese characters better. The writing sheets illustrate the correct stroke order of each character. Grid lines and traceable characters are also provided to help students trace and copy characters until they are able to write them independently. The teacher may assign additional character writing practice according to learning emphasis and needs.

• Review Units

Two Review units are provided after every five lessons in the Workbook. They give students the opportunity to review and reflect on their knowledge and progress, and reinforce what they have learned. Teachers may have students work on these units individually as homework, or go over them together in class.

The Workbook is designed to enable students to complete all exercises independently, either in class, or at home. Students should not have to spend more than 15 minutes on each page. Teachers may also wish to encourage students to spend 10 minutes a day on the Sentence Quiz exercises in the CD-ROM.

Table of Contents

1

我的学校
My School

1 Translate the following words into Chinese and fill in each box below with the appropriate Chinese word and its *pinyin*. Each word can only be used once.

> **A** restroom **B** dining hall **C** stadium **D** library
> **E** office **F** classroom **G** gym **H** principal's office

① 中午，我和同学去 ☐ 吃饭。

② 我喜欢去 ☐ 看书。

③ 男 ☐ 在教室旁边，你向前走就可以看到了。

④ 弟弟在学校打架，校长要爸爸去 ☐ 找他。

⑤ 晴天，我喜欢在 ☐ 跑步；雨天，我喜欢在
☐ 打球。

⑥ 我要找谢老师，请问老师 ☐ 在哪里？

⑦ 我要上中文课，你知道中文 ☐ 在哪里吗？

2 Study the floor plan below and answer the following questions.

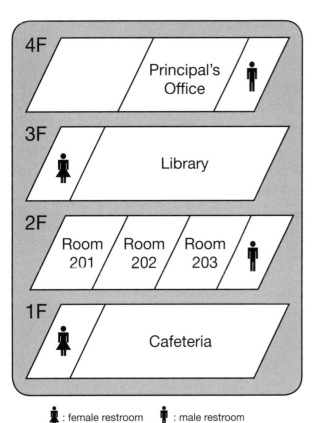

4F — Principal's Office | male restroom

3F — female restroom | Library

2F — Room 201 | Room 202 | Room 203 | male restroom

1F — female restroom | Cafeteria

👧 : female restroom   🧍 : male restroom

1 餐厅在哪里？

_____

2 图书馆楼下有什么？

_____

3 203 教室右边有什么？

_____

4 图书馆在几楼？

校长室也在那里吗？

_____

_____

3 Go to *Exercise > Sentence Quiz* in your 🔘Go400 to take the quiz. Choose the best two results.

TYPING RECORDS

Record 1	Date	Accurate Spelling per Minute	Three Most Common Mistakes (Character)
	Level	Time Elapsed	

Record 2	Date	Accurate Spelling per Minute	Three Most Common Mistakes (Character)
	Level	Time Elapsed	

4 Write ✓ in the box next to the sentence if it is correct, and ✗ if it is incorrect. Then write the correct sentence in the space provided.

① ☐ 你知道谁在家吗？

　➥ _____

② ☐ 办公室怎么去吗？

　➥ _____

③ ☐ 你知道女厕所在哪里吗？

　➥ _____

④ ☐ 妈妈买了什么吗？

　➥ _____

⑤ ☐ 医院在那里？

　➥ _____

⑥ ☐ 请问从这里到餐厅怎么走？

　➥ _____

⑦ ☐ 他知道学校在哪里？

　➥ _____

⑧ ☐ 我不知道他在哪里吗？

　➥ _____

⑨ ☐ 办公室在二楼，图书馆也在那里吗？

　➥ _____

5 Fill in the blanks with the words provided. Each word can only be used once.

> **A** 上楼　**B** 下楼　**C** 楼上
> **D** 楼下　**E** 有　**F** 在

① 你在三楼，我在一楼，我在＿＿＿＿＿＿等你。

② 请问＿＿＿＿＿＿有厕所吗？

③ 我的教室在二楼，图书馆在四楼。我常常＿＿＿＿＿＿看书。

④ 谢老师的办公室在楼下，请你＿＿＿＿＿＿找他。

⑤ 你们学校＿＿＿＿＿＿运动场吗？

⑥ 运动场＿＿＿＿＿＿哪里？

6 Go to *Exercise > Sentence Quiz* in your **Go 400** to take the quiz. Choose the best two results.

TYPING RECORDS		Date	Accurate Spelling per Minute	Three Most Common Mistakes (Character)
	Record 1			
		Level	Time Elapsed	
	Record 2	Date	Accurate Spelling per Minute	Three Most Common Mistakes (Character)
		Level	Time Elapsed	

7 Practice the strokes to write the characters.

lóu	shì	zhī	dào	bàn
楼	室	知	道	办

男厕所在二＿＿＿的教＿＿＿旁边。
　　　　　lóu　　　　shì

你＿＿＿＿＿＿＿＿＿公室在哪里吗？
　zhī　　dào　　bàn

楼楼楼楼楼楼楼楼楼楼楼楼

楼楼楼

室室室室室室室室室

室室室

知知知知知知知知

知知知

道道道道道道道道道道道

道道道

办办办办

办办办

8a Read what Jeff and Lily have to say about their school.

我们学校的图书馆在体育馆左边，图书馆的左边有餐厅。校长室和老师办公室在运动场的左边，办公室在二楼，校长室在一楼。我最喜欢去体育馆打球。

Lily

Jeff

我们学校不大，一到学校就会看到运动场，运动场后面还有体育馆。校长室和老师办公室在运动场的旁边，校长室在楼下，老师办公室在楼上。体育馆的右边有教室，左边有图书馆。图书馆是我最喜欢的地方。

8b According to the above accounts, decide which of the following floor plans represent Jeff and Lily's schools. Label them "Jeff" and "Lily" respectively in the boxes provided. In the correct floor plan, circle the area they enjoy being at most.

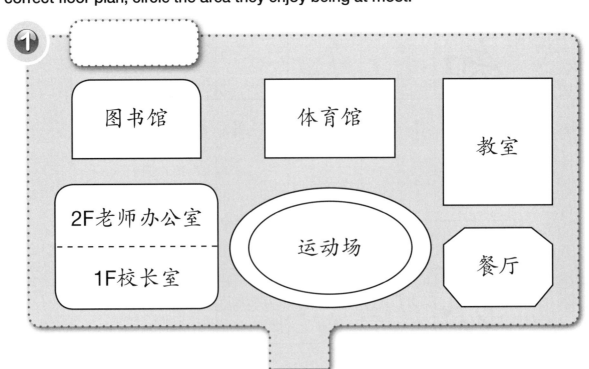

① [ ]

图书馆　　体育馆　　教室

2F老师办公室 / 1F校长室　　运动场　　餐厅

②

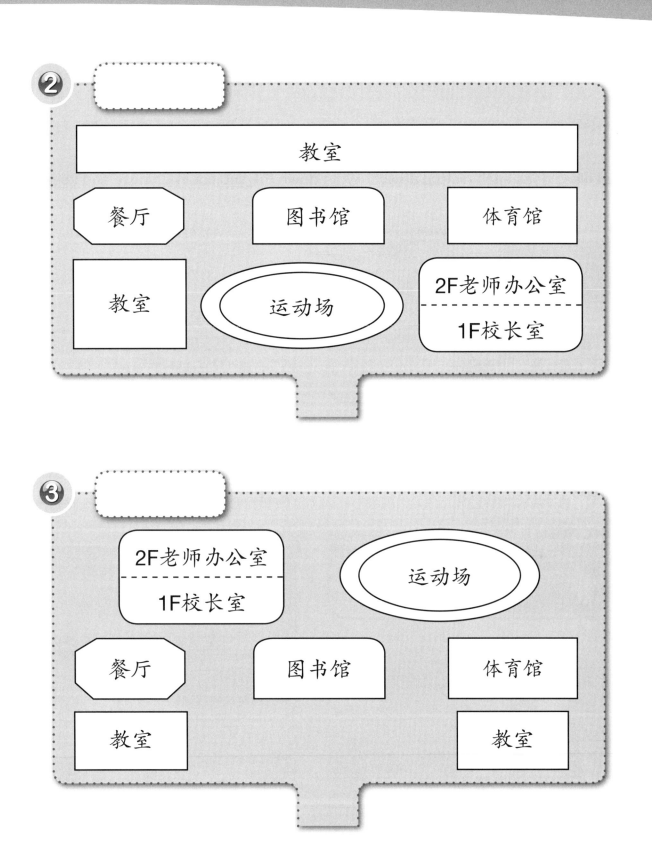

教室		
餐厅	图书馆	体育馆
教室	运动场	2F老师办公室 1F校长室

③

2F老师办公室 1F校长室	运动场	
餐厅	图书馆	体育馆
教室		教室

我的学科
My Subjects

1 What class does each picture depict? Write down the subject in Chinese and its *pinyin*.

① Chinese

数学

Pinyin

shù xué

② Chinese

Pinyin

③ Chinese

Pinyin

④ Chinese

Pinyin

⑤ Chinese

Pinyin

⑥ Chinese

Pinyin

2 Circle the extra word in each of the following sentences.

① 我爸爸不会开车，他什么车都开得很好。

② 老师送了一两本书给我，那本书很好看。

③ 数学、科学和史地，你最喜欢哪一学科？

④ 这个问题太难了，我答不错了。

⑤ 我上课很认识真，我的成绩很好。

⑥ 你知道是谁是王老师吗？

⑦ 中文歌、英文歌，什么歌都真好听。

3 Go to *Exercise > Sentence Quiz* in your ⊙[Go 400] to take the quiz. Choose the best two results.

TYPING RECORDS		Date	Accurate Spelling per Minute	Three Most Common Mistakes (Character)
	Record 1			
		Level	Time Elapsed	
	Record 2	Date	Accurate Spelling per Minute	Three Most Common Mistakes (Character)
		Level	Time Elapsed	

4 Rewrite the following sentences using the structure "……，什么都……".

① 他买的衣服、鞋子、书和背包都很贵。

他买的东西，什么都很贵。

② 学校的球队、乐队、啦啦队和学生会都很好玩。

③ 我喜欢中文、数学、科学、史地、美劳和音乐。

5 Rearrange the phrases to form a coherent sentence. In the boxes, write the corresponding letters in the right order.

①
Ⓐ 谁可以教我？

Ⓑ 小明的数学不错，

Ⓒ 这题数学我答错了，

Ⓓ 他可以教你。

➡ (A: ☐ ☐)
(B: ☐ ☐)

②
Ⓐ 我的新学校有新教室、

Ⓑ 还有新校长和新老师，

Ⓒ 什么都是新的。

Ⓓ 新大楼、新图书馆，

➡ (☐ ☐ ☐ ☐)

6 Fill in the blanks with appropriate words.

> **Ⓐ** 对　　　**Ⓑ** 不对　　　**Ⓒ** 对不对　　　**Ⓓ** 错　　　**Ⓔ** 不错

① "99 x 13 = (1287)"，这题你答_____了。

② "325 ÷ 27 = (15)"，这题你答_____了。

③ 你打_____电话了，这里没有你要找的人。

④ 你唱歌唱得真_____。

⑤ 你看我写得_____？

⑥ 我大考考得还_____，我很开心。

⑦ _____，你答错了！

7 Go to *Exercise > Sentence Quiz* in your **Go400** to take the quiz. Choose the best two results.

TYPING RECORDS		Date	Accurate Spelling per Minute	Three Most Common Mistakes (Character)
	Record 1			
		Level	Time Elapsed	
	Record 2	Date	Accurate Spelling per Minute	Three Most Common Mistakes (Character)
		Level	Time Elapsed	

8 Practice the strokes to write the characters.

rèn	shí	liàn	xí	cuò
认	识	练	习	错

想＿＿＿ ＿＿＿中文字，要多看、多＿＿＿ ＿＿＿。
rèn　　shi　　　　　　　　　　　　　liàn　　xí

常常＿＿＿ ＿＿＿，就不会写＿＿＿字。
　　　liàn　　xí　　　　　　　　　cuò

认 认 认 认

认	认	认			

识 识 识 识 识 识 识

识	识	识			

练 练 练 练 练 练 练 练

练	练	练			

习 习 习

习	习	习			

错 错 错 错 错 错 错 错 错 错 错 错 错

错	错	错			

9 Jeff (小明) talks about his weekly schedule below. Can you figure out when does he have Art class?

① 从星期一到星期五，我都要上课。每天上三科，每科都不一样。

② 我要上的学科一共有八科，我最喜欢史地、科学和体育。

③ 一个星期要上一次美劳、一次电脑和一次音乐。

④ 星期一、星期三和星期五，我要上英文；星期二和星期四，我要上科学。

⑤ 除了星期三，每天都有体育课。

⑥ 每天要上的课很多，星期二的课我都喜欢。

⑦ 星期一和星期二，有两个一样的课。

⑧ 有电脑课的那一天，也有数学课。

⑨ 有科学课的那一天，没有音乐课。

TIP
It would be easier for you to derive the answer if you arrange the above information into the format of a timetable.

➡ 星期＿＿＿，小明要上美劳课。

过生日
Celebrating Birthdays

1 Fill in the blanks with the words provided.

> **A** 庆祝   **B** 生日   **C** 健康   **D** 更
> **E** 帮忙   **F** 礼物   **G** 快乐   **H** 希望

① 祝你生日 _____。

② 奶奶八十岁了，我们要帮她 _____。

③ 希望你喜欢我送你的 _____。

④ 明天的比赛，_____ 我们会赢。

⑤ 我的成绩不错，可是他的成绩 _____ 好。

⑥ 多运动，身体就会 _____。

⑦ 你的衣服洗不完，要不要我 _____？

⑧ 下个星期妈妈过 _____，我们要送什么礼物给她？

2 Complete the following dialogues by checking the box next to the appropriate sentence.

① **A**：你真高，你是你家最高的人吗？

B：
- ☐ 不是，我很高，可是我爸爸更高。
- ☐ 不是，爸爸更高，可是我是家里最高的人。

② **A**：下个月七号是你的生日，你想在哪里庆祝？

B：
- ☐ 和家人一起庆祝生日是我的希望。
- ☐ 我希望和家人一起在家里过生日。

③ **A**：
- ☐ 有了你的帮忙，球队打得更好了。
- ☐ 明天球队要开始练习了，希望你能来帮忙。

B：没问题，我可以帮你的忙。

3 Go to *Exercise > Sentence Quiz* in your [Go 400] to take the quiz. Choose the best two results.

TYPING RECORDS		Date	Accurate Spelling per Minute	Three Most Common Mistakes (Character)
Record 1				
		Level	Time Elapsed	
Record 2		Date	Accurate Spelling per Minute	Three Most Common Mistakes (Character)
		Level	Time Elapsed	

4 Study the e-mail correspondence below and answer the following questions.

From: Jeff
To: Daguan
Subject: Birthday Invitation

大关：

明天是我十六岁生日，妈妈会做蛋糕和好吃的食物。我想请你和小贵下午一起来我家玩，你可以来吗？

希望你能来！

小明

From: Daguan
To: Jeff
Subject: Re: Birthday Invitation

小明：

谢谢你请我去你家，和你一起过生日。我明天得和哥哥一起参加棒球比赛，比赛完了我就去你家。希望球赛能早一点儿比完。

我想送礼物给你，你希望我送你什么礼物？

祝你生日快乐！

大关

❶ （ ） 明天是（❶ 小明 ❷ 小贵 ❸ 大关）的生日。

❷ （ ） 明天大关会去小明家吗？（❶ 大关要参加球赛，不能去小明家。 ❷ 早一点儿比赛，就会去小明家。 ❸ 比赛完了，就会去小明家。）

❸ （ ） 谁会帮小明做蛋糕？（❶ 大关 ❷ 小明的妈妈 ❸ 大关的妈妈）

❹ （ ） 大关要送什么礼物给小明？（❶ 棒球 ❷ 蛋糕 ❸ 大关没说）

5 Write ✓ in the box next to the sentence if it is correct, and ✗ if it is incorrect. Write the correct sentence in the space provided.

1 ◯ 多练习，就可以学得更好。

➡ _____

2 ◯ 爸爸喜欢吃面包，他说面包更好吃。

➡ _____

3 ◯ 今天105°F，昨天98°F，今天很热，昨天更热。

➡ _____

4 ◯ 我希望明年长得比今年高。

➡ _____

5 ◯ 我们比赛赢了，大家要一起过。

➡ _____

6 ◯ 祝福明天不会下雨。

➡ _____

6 Go to *Exercise > Sentence Quiz* in your ⬤ Go400 to take the quiz. Choose the best two results.

TYPING RECORDS

Record 1	Date	Accurate Spelling per Minute	Three Most Common Mistakes (Character)
	Level	Time Elapsed	

Record 2	Date	Accurate Spelling per Minute	Three Most Common Mistakes (Character)
	Level	Time Elapsed	

过生日　17

7 Practice the strokes to write the characters.

xī	wàng	gèng	jiàn	kāng
希	望	更	健	康

我爱爸爸、妈妈，我＿＿＿ ＿＿＿他们天天开
　　　　　　　　　xī　　wàng

心，＿＿＿ ＿＿＿ ＿＿＿他们身体＿＿＿ ＿＿＿。
　　gèng　　xī　　wàng　　　　　　jiàn　　kāng

希 希 希 希 希 希 希

希	希	希			

望 望 望 望 望 望 望 望 望 望

望	望	望			

更 更 更 更 更 更 更

更	更	更			

健 健 健 健 健 健 健 健 健 健

健	健	健			

康 康 康 康 康 康 康 康 康 康

康	康	康			

8 Using your information from the "Let's Do It" activity (Page 36) in the Go400 Textbook, complete the sentences below.

1

今年＿＿＿＿＿月＿＿＿＿＿日是我＿＿＿＿＿岁生日，大家祝

福我＿＿＿＿＿＿＿＿＿＿＿＿＿＿＿＿＿＿＿＿＿＿＿＿＿＿＿＿＿＿

＿＿＿＿＿＿＿＿＿＿＿＿＿＿＿＿＿＿＿＿＿＿＿＿＿＿＿＿＿＿＿＿

我希望这一年＿＿＿＿＿＿＿＿＿＿＿＿＿＿＿＿＿＿＿＿＿＿＿＿

＿＿＿＿＿＿＿＿＿＿＿＿＿＿＿＿＿＿＿＿＿＿＿＿＿＿＿＿＿＿＿＿

2

＿＿＿＿＿月＿＿＿＿＿日是＿＿＿＿＿＿＿＿＿＿＿＿＿的生日，

我祝福＿＿＿＿＿＿＿＿＿＿＿＿＿＿＿＿＿＿＿＿＿＿＿＿＿＿＿＿

＿＿＿＿＿＿＿＿＿＿＿＿＿＿＿＿＿＿＿＿＿＿＿＿＿＿＿＿＿＿＿＿

3

＿＿＿＿＿月＿＿＿＿＿日是＿＿＿＿＿＿＿＿＿＿＿＿＿的生日，

我祝福＿＿＿＿＿＿＿＿＿＿＿＿＿＿＿＿＿＿＿＿＿＿＿＿＿＿＿＿

＿＿＿＿＿＿＿＿＿＿＿＿＿＿＿＿＿＿＿＿＿＿＿＿＿＿＿＿＿＿＿＿

养小动物
Keeping Pets

1 Combine the letters to form the *pinyin* of the word that describes each picture. Write the *pinyin* and the Chinese words in the table below.

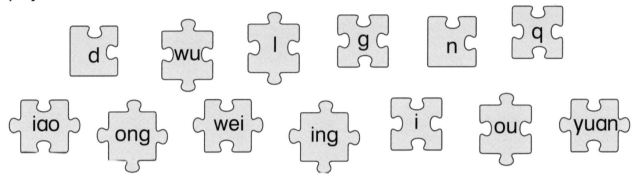

Picture	*Pinyin*	Chinese
①		
②		
③		
④		
⑤		

2 Circle the odd one out in each row.

① Ⓐ 条　Ⓑ 它　Ⓒ 张　Ⓓ 只

② Ⓐ 它　Ⓑ 你　Ⓒ 我　Ⓓ 他

③ Ⓐ 好看　Ⓑ 可爱　Ⓒ 难看　Ⓓ 美丽

④ Ⓐ 小鱼　Ⓑ 小猫　Ⓒ 小动物　Ⓓ 小鸟

⑤ Ⓐ 养　Ⓑ 喂　Ⓒ 照顾　Ⓓ 大小便

⑥ Ⓐ 清理　Ⓑ 练习　Ⓒ 扫落叶　Ⓓ 洗衣服

⑦ Ⓐ 红花　Ⓑ 白猫　Ⓒ 黑狗　Ⓓ 红鱼

3 Go to *Exercise > Sentence Quiz* in your ⬤Go400 to take the quiz. Choose the best two results.

TYPING RECORDS		Date	Accurate Spelling per Minute	Three Most Common Mistakes (Character)
	Record 1			
		Level	Time Elapsed	
	Record 2	Date	Accurate Spelling per Minute	Three Most Common Mistakes (Character)
		Level	Time Elapsed	

4 Choose the appropriate questions and answers below to create a relevant dialogue for each picture.

①
😀： ＿＿＿＿
😀： ＿＿＿＿
😀： ＿＿＿＿

②
😀： ＿A＿
😀： ＿＿＿＿
😀： ＿＿＿＿
😀： ＿＿＿＿

③
😀： ＿＿＿＿
😀： ＿B＿
😀： ＿＿＿＿
😀： ＿＿＿＿

Ⓐ 你有没有养小动物？

Ⓑ 对。它是爷爷送我的生日礼物。

Ⓒ 除了我照顾小狗，我弟弟也会帮忙。
我弟弟每天带它去散步。

Ⓓ 我在家里养了很多不同的鱼。

Ⓔ 早上我喂，下午爸爸喂。

Ⓕ 每天是谁喂鱼的？

Ⓖ 用心就很容易。

Ⓗ 我家的花园里有很多花。

Ⓘ 种花容易吗？

Ⓙ 你怎么有时间照顾它？

Ⓚ 这只小狗真可爱！它是你家的狗吗？

5 Fill in the blanks with the words and phrases provided.

> Ⓐ 鸟在唱歌　Ⓑ 狗在后面跑　Ⓒ 比我们忙
>
> Ⓓ 买了六只　Ⓔ 看谁跑得快　Ⓕ 鸟
>
> Ⓖ 喂它们　Ⓗ 养了五条鱼

爸爸喜欢_____，所以他养了三只。我们每天都可以听到_____。哥哥喜欢狗，他喜欢带狗到公园跑步，哥哥在前面跑，_____，_____。妹妹说，鱼最可爱，所以她_____。妈妈什么都没养，可是她_____。她每天要_____，还要帮小狗、小鸟清理大小便。

Go 400

In the CD, type the complete passage into the section "Exercise > Teacher's Assignment". Print it out and record the time spent on the exercise.

Time Spent: _____

6 Go to *Exercise > Sentence Quiz* in your **Go 400** to take the quiz. Choose the best two results.

TYPING RECORDS

		Date	Accurate Spelling per Minute	Three Most Common Mistakes (Character)
Record **1**				
		Level	Time Elapsed	
		Date	Accurate Spelling per Minute	Three Most Common Mistakes (Character)
Record **2**				
		Level	Time Elapsed	

7 Practice the strokes to write the characters.

māo	qīng	gǒu	niǎo	yú
猫	清	狗	鸟	鱼

我每天早上要帮＿＿ ＿＿理大小便，下午
　　　　　　　　māo　　qīng

要带＿＿去散步。家里还养了＿＿和＿＿。
　　gǒu　　　　　　　　　　niǎo　　　yú

猫 猫 猫 猫 猫 猫 猫 猫 猫 猫 猫

猫	猫	猫				

清 清 清 清 清 清 清 清 清 清 清

清	清	清				

狗 狗 狗 狗 狗 狗 狗 狗

狗	狗	狗				

鸟 鸟 鸟 鸟 鸟

鸟	鸟	鸟				

鱼 鱼 鱼 鱼 鱼 鱼 鱼 鱼

鱼	鱼	鱼				

8 While looking after a pet demands much time and effort, it can also be an unforgettable experience. In the box below, write down the pet you would like to have. Choose four categories and write down how you would handle, or would feel about handling, those demands. If you already have a pet, you may also use this exercise to share your experience as a pet owner.

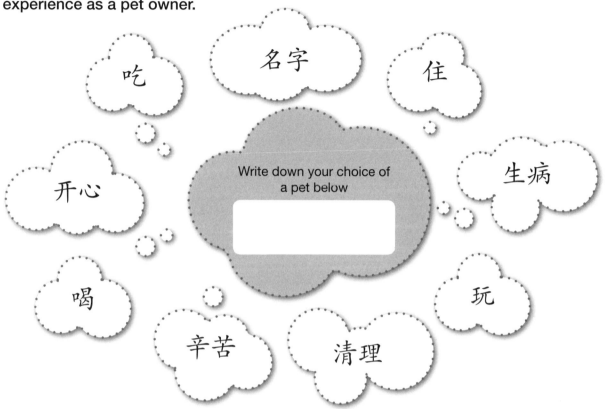

Example:

| 玩 | ➡ | 我想养一只狗，我会带它去公园玩球。 |
| 名字 | ➡ | 我要叫我的狗"阳光"。 |

① [   ] ➡ _____

② [   ] ➡ _____

③ [   ] ➡ _____

④ [   ] ➡ _____

我的假期
My Vacation

1 Translate the English terms into Chinese and write down the *pinyin*.

	English	Chinese	*Pinyin*
1	weekend		
2	summer vacation		
3	winter vacation		
4	vacation		
5	have a part-time job		
6	travel		
7	only		
8	tired		

2 Choose the appropriate answers from the following box to complete the dialogues below. Write the corresponding letters in the blanks. Each option can only be used once.

> **A** 今年暑假有几天？
>
> **B** 你想去哪里打工？
>
> **C** 这个周末你要做什么？
>
> **D** 你什么时候开始放暑假？
>
> **E** 寒假你会做什么？

1 ☺: _____ ☺: 我有时去旅行，有时去打工。

2 ☺: _____ ☺: 我从六月十五日开始放暑假。

3 ☺: _____ ☺: 我要在家帮爸妈的忙。

4 ☺: _____ ☺: 我想去学校打工。

5 ☺: _____ ☺: 一共有六十二天。

3 Go to *Exercise > Sentence Quiz* in your 〔Go 400〕 to take the quiz. Choose the best two results.

		Date	Accurate Spelling per Minute	Three Most Common Mistakes (Character)
TYPING RECORDS	**Record 1**			
		Level	Time Elapsed	
	Record 2	Date	Accurate Spelling per Minute	Three Most Common Mistakes (Character)
		Level	Time Elapsed	

4 Complete the dialogues with the clues provided in the corresponding pictures.

①

Ⓐ： _____

Ⓑ： 我想去餐厅打工。

②

Ⓐ： 你想喝什么？

Ⓑ： 我_____，可是_____

_____（只有／不够）

③

Ⓐ： 看！这里有100块钱。

Ⓑ： _____

_____（别人／拿）

④

Ⓐ： _____，

你来我家玩，好不好？

Ⓑ： 我会去的。我想送你一个礼物，

_____（还是）

Ⓐ： 棒球和帽子我都喜欢。

5 The three sentences in each set contain a common word that has been underlined. Identify the sentence in which the word has a different meaning from the other two.

① (3)　❶ 明天还要上课，电视<u>别</u>看得太晚。

　　　　　❷ 这本书太贵了，我要买<u>别</u>的。

　　　　　❸ 五点的节目很精彩，<u>别</u>走开(leave)。
　　　　　　　　　　　　　　　　zǒu kāi

② (2)　❶ <u>别</u>人都说我家的狗真可爱。
　　　 3

　　　　　❷ <u>别</u>的笔你都可以拿，只有这支不行。

　　　　　❸ <u>别</u>忘了明天是奶奶生日，我们要一起庆祝。

③ (2)　❶ 表弟<u>长</u>大了，他学会做很多事。

　　　　　❷ 教室里有一张<u>长</u>桌子。

　　　　　❸ 我喜欢<u>长</u>假期，因为可以去旅行。

④ (1)　❶ 张<u>开</u>眼睛，我们可以看书。

　　　　　❷ 我们比赛赢了，真<u>开</u>心！

　　　　　❸ 我一回家就打<u>开</u>电视看新闻。

6 Go to *Exercise > Sentence Quiz* in your 〔Go 400〕 to take the quiz. Choose the best two results.

	Date	Accurate Spelling per Minute	Three Most Common Mistakes (Character)
Record 1			
	Level	Time Elapsed	
	Date	Accurate Spelling per Minute	Three Most Common Mistakes (Character)
Record 2			
	Level	Time Elapsed	

TYPING RECORDS

7 Practice the strokes to write the characters.

jià	gōng	fàng	bié	lèi
假	工	放	别	累

今年暑＿＿＿，我想去打＿＿＿。爸妈说："＿＿＿

　　　jià　　　　　　　　　gōng　　　　　　　　　　　fàng

＿＿＿打＿＿＿很好，可是＿＿＿太＿＿＿了。"
jià　　　gōng　　　　　　　　bié　　　lèi

假假假假假假假假假假假
假 假 假

工 工 工
工 工 工

放放放放放放放放
放 放 放

别别别别别别别
别 别 别

累累累累累累累累累累累
累 累 累

8

Use the pictures to help Jeff (小明) write his travelogue with the words provided. The travelogue should comprise at least five sentences.

		zhōng guó			
旅行 /	堂哥 /	中国 /	大楼 /	奶奶 /	狗
散步 /	公园 /	美丽 /	吃 /	很多 /	开心

我的假期！

我还有我的很朋肢旅行搭飞机。我们只有旅行中国，因为我放两假。我，我的朋友还有奶奶走路。

我们走路奶奶的狗。我们玩游戏奶奶的狗，她可爱！

REVIEW 1

1a
Circle the odd one out in each row and fill in the boxes below according to the *pinyin* tones.

1. Ⓐ 假期　Ⓑ 春假　Ⓒ 周末　Ⓓ 旅行

2. Ⓐ 不错　Ⓑ 错了　Ⓒ 不对　Ⓓ 不是

3. Ⓐ 快乐　Ⓑ 健康　Ⓒ 幸福　Ⓓ 庆祝

4. Ⓐ 数学　Ⓑ 学科　Ⓒ 音乐　Ⓓ 地理

5. Ⓐ 右转　Ⓑ 左转　Ⓒ 楼上　Ⓓ 上楼

1b
From the list of words above, identify:

(i)　words made up of two characters of the same tone.

快乐 ＿＿＿＿、＿＿＿＿、＿＿＿＿

(ii)　words in which the first character is in the first tone and the second character is in the fourth tone.

春假 ＿＿＿＿、＿＿＿＿、＿＿＿＿

(iii)　words in which the first character is in the fourth tone and the second character is in the second tone.

幸福 ＿＿＿＿、＿＿＿＿、＿＿＿＿

2 The following is a continuous dialogue. Check the boxes next to the most appropriate options to complete the dialogue. Complete Question 4 according to the picture below.

① : 今年的寒假，你要做什么？

⬜ 每年的寒假，我都会去旅行。

⬜ 寒假我要去中国看外公外婆。
zhōng guó

⬜ 我今年暑假去打工，寒假也想去打工。

② : ⬜ 我外公外婆也住在中国。我们一起去中国旅行，好不好？

⬜ 寒假很短，别去打工了！我们一起去旅行，好不好？

: 你想去哪里旅行？

③ : 电视节目说，加拿大(Canada)很美。我想去加拿大旅行。
jiā ná dà

⬜ 我们什么时候去旅行？

⬜ 你知道去加拿大要多少钱吗？

⬜ 我也想去加拿大，你要去几天？

④ : 我们一起来看一看。去加拿大要

_____

: _____

$852

3 According to the pictures, form questions for answers provided.

①

 : _____

 : 不是，它是奶奶送我的生日礼物。

 : _____

 : 它叫小白。

②

 : _____

 : 会，小白喜欢跳上跳下，常常和我一起玩球。

③

 : _____

 : 不行，它只能吃猫吃的东西。

④

 : _____

 : 是我，我天天帮猫清理大小便。不帮它清理大小便，它会不健康。

4 Translate B's answer into Chinese. You may use the helping words provided below.

> **Ⓐ** 还不错　**Ⓑ** 更多　**Ⓒ** 快乐
> **Ⓓ** 什么……都……　**Ⓔ** 有

① **Ⓐ**：你今年选了几个学科?

　　Ⓑ：I have selected seven subjects this year—English, Chinese, Mathematics, Computing, History, Music, and Physical Education.

(Translation) _____

② **Ⓐ**：我看你选了电脑课，电脑课好玩吗?

　　Ⓑ：It is not bad. However, it is very difficult.

(Translation) _____

③ **Ⓐ**：你选七个学科，不会很累吗?

　　Ⓑ：No. I enjoy all my subjects so I find my lessons very enjoyable.

(Translation) _____

④ **Ⓐ**：你是选最多学科的人吗?

　　Ⓑ：No. Jeff (小明) is taking eight subjects. He has more classes than me.

(Translation) _____

5 Read the following text and choose the correct sentence in each question.

我的新学校就在我家附近，走十五分钟就到了。

我们一进学校，就可以看到图书馆。学生上课的教室在图书馆后面。除了音乐课和体育课，每一个学科的教室都在二楼。我们上音乐课时得下楼，老师办公室和校长室也在那里。

我们学校只有体育馆，没有运动场。体育馆在教室右边，大家天天在那里上体育课。

今年是学校五十岁生日，我们有很多庆祝活动，有运动比赛，也有音乐表演^{biǎo yǎn}*。学校还会找以前的学生回来，一起帮学校庆祝。

我们班要参加那天的运动比赛，希望我们可以赢，更希望那一天快一点儿来。

*表演 performance

① ( ) ❶ 作者(author)的学校是新的。 ❷ 作者家离学校很近。 ❸ 作者每天要走路十五分钟。

② ( ) ❶ 作者的教室后面有图书馆。 ❷ 音乐教室在一楼。 ❸ 老师办公室在音乐教室旁边。

③ ( ) ❶ 教室的右边是体育馆。 ❷ 大家天天在运动场上体育课。 ❸ 教室离校门(gates)很近。

④ ( ) ❶ 作者最希望学校生日那天快一点儿来。 ❷ 作者赢了学校的运动比赛。 ❸ 音乐课和体育课都是学校的庆祝活动。

6 **Read the following information. What color do you think Jeff's hat is?**

> 教室有三顶^{*}红帽子和两顶白帽子。老师帮小贵、大关和小明(Jeff) 戴上帽子。他们可以看见别人的帽子，可是看不到自己的帽子是什么颜色^{*}的。

_{dǐng}

_{yán sè}

*顶 (a measure word for headgear)
*颜色 color

同学问小贵："你戴的帽子是什么颜色的？"

小贵看看大关和小明，说："我不知道。"

同学问大关："你戴的帽子是什么颜色的？"

大关想一想，说："我也不知道。"

同学问小明："你戴的帽子是什么颜色的？"

小明说："我知道了，我戴的帽子是_____色的。"

TIP

There are three people but only two white hats in the classroom. If 小贵 and 大关 wear either a red or white hat, there will be two red hats and one white hat left. Following this line of deduction, under what circumstances would Jeff be able to determine the color of his hat? Work out the possible combinations to deduce the answer.

我家房间
Rooms in My Home

1a Write the names of the rooms depicted in Chinese and their *pinyin* in the boxes below.

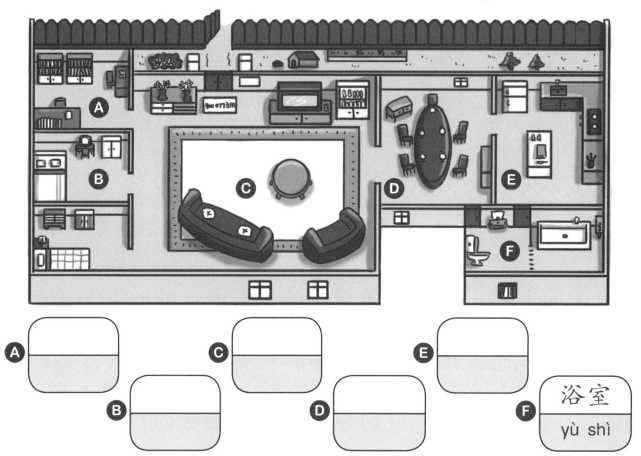

A

B

C

D

E

F 浴室
yù shì

1b Fill in the blanks according to the floor plan above.

① _____的右边是_____，我常常和爸爸在那里做菜。

② 客人来了，我们一起在_____聊天、看电视。

       liáo tiān

③ _____的旁边是_____，我喜欢在那里看书、做功课。

2 Fill in the blanks with the appropriate measure words provided below.

> **A** 一步一步　　**B** 一家一家　　**C** 一只一只
>
> **D** 一条一条　　**E** 一本一本　　**F** 一个一个
>
> **G** 一题一题　　**H** 一课一课

① 我喜欢鱼，爸爸＿＿＿＿＿＿买给我。

② 小明不知道我说的餐厅在哪里，他＿＿＿＿＿＿找。

③ 姑姑买了很多东西，她＿＿＿＿＿＿拿给我看。

④ 外公外婆常常一起散步，他们＿＿＿＿＿＿小心走。

⑤ 老师问了很多问题，我要＿＿＿＿＿＿用心回答。

⑥ 新课本有十课，我会＿＿＿＿＿＿认真地学。

3 Go to *Exercise > Sentence Quiz* in your **Go 400** to take the quiz. Choose the best two results.

TYPING RECORDS		Date	Accurate Spelling per Minute	Three Most Common Mistakes (Character)
	Record 1			
		Level	Time Elapsed	
		Date	Accurate Spelling per Minute	Three Most Common Mistakes (Character)
	Record 2			
		Level	Time Elapsed	

4 Complete each dialogue according to the corresponding pictures.

😀： _____

😑： 小贵家的客厅有桌子、_____

🙂： 他们在做什么？

😀： _____

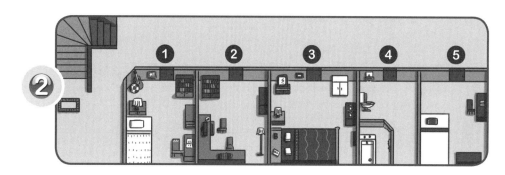

❶ 我的睡房
❷ 书房
❸ 爸妈的睡房
❹ 厕所
❺ 客房

🙂： _____

😑： 我的睡房在二楼。

🙂： 从你的睡房到厕所，会经过什么？

😑： _____

🙂： _____

😑： 客人可以睡在客房。从我的睡房出来向右走，客房就在厕所右边。

5 Describe each picture with a sentence. The sentence must include the action, location, and time as depicted in the picture.

一放学回家，我＿＿＿＿＿＿＿＿＿＿

＿＿＿＿＿＿＿＿＿＿＿＿＿＿＿＿＿＿

洗过澡，＿＿＿＿＿＿＿＿＿＿＿＿＿

＿＿＿＿＿＿＿＿＿＿＿＿＿＿＿＿＿＿

＿＿＿＿＿＿＿＿＿＿＿＿＿＿＿＿＿＿

＿＿＿＿＿＿＿＿＿＿＿＿＿＿＿＿＿＿

6 Go to *Exercise > Sentence Quiz* in your to take the quiz. Choose the best two results.

TYPING RECORDS		Date	Accurate Spelling per Minute	Three Most Common Mistakes (Character)
	Record 1			
		Level	Time Elapsed	
	Record 2	Date	Accurate Spelling per Minute	Three Most Common Mistakes (Character)
		Level	Time Elapsed	

7 Practice the strokes to write the characters.

fáng	jiān	dōng	xī	zuò
房	间	东	西	坐

我的＿＿＿＿ ＿＿＿＿有很多书，还有很多好玩的
　　　　fáng　　jiān

＿＿＿＿ ＿＿＿＿。我喜欢＿＿＿在＿＿＿＿ ＿＿＿＿里看书。
dōng　　　xi　　　　　　　　zuò　　　　fáng　　jiān

房 房 房 房 房 房 房 房

房 房 房

间 间 间 间 间 间 间

间 间 间

东 东 东 东 东

东 东 东

西 西 西 西 西 西

西 西 西

坐 坐 坐 坐 坐 坐 坐

坐 坐 坐

8a

Look at the pictures and fill in the blanks with the character's actions.

Ⓐ 洗过澡，我＿＿＿＿＿吃早餐。

Ⓑ 看半个小时的书，我再＿＿＿＿＿＿。

Ⓒ 早上七点，我一起床就去＿＿＿＿＿。

Ⓓ 八点，我自己去＿＿＿＿＿。

Ⓔ 晚上九点半，我喜欢在床上＿＿＿＿＿。

Ⓕ 下午放学回家，我帮妈妈＿＿＿＿＿。

Ⓖ 吃过晚餐，我帮忙＿＿＿＿＿饭桌，

Ⓗ 再＿＿＿＿＿到书房做功课。

8b

Rearrange the above descriptions in chronological order and write their corresponding letters in the boxes below.

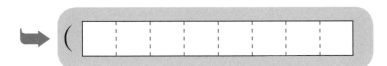

7

我用筷子
Using Chopsticks

1 Locate the numbered items in the following picture. In the table below, state the item and how many of each item there are with the correct measure word.

	Chinese	How many of the items are there?		Chinese	How many of the items are there?
1	杯子	一个杯子	5		
2			6		
3			7		
4			8		

2 With the helping words provided, translate the following sentences into Chinese.

> **A** 拿　　**B** 放　　**C** 用　　**D** 喝　　**E** 有　　**F** 把

1 I put the knife in the kitchen.

_____

2 Younger Brother uses the spoon to drink soup.

_____

3 I drank three glasses of milk yesterday.

_____

4 There are vegetables on the plate and soup in the bowl.

_____

5 I can use both a pair of chopsticks and a fork.

_____

3 Go to *Exercise > Sentence Quiz* in your [Go 400] to take the quiz. Choose the best two results.

TYPING RECORDS		Date	Accurate Spelling per Minute	Three Most Common Mistakes (Character)
	Record 1			
		Level	Time Elapsed	
		Date	Accurate Spelling per Minute	Three Most Common Mistakes (Character)
	Record 2			
		Level	Time Elapsed	

我用筷子　　45

4 Rewrite the following sentences by incorporating "把" in them.

① 吃完饭，妹妹洗了碗。

吃完饭，妹妹把碗洗好了。

② 小贵写完作业了。

_____

③ 我喝完汤了。

_____

④ 早上妈妈洗好衣服了。

_____

5 Go to *Exercise > Sentence Quiz* in your 〔Go 400〕 to take the quiz. Choose the best two results.

TYPING RECORDS		Date	Accurate Spelling per Minute	Three Most Common Mistakes (Character)
	Record 1			
		Level	Time Elapsed	
	Record 2	Date	Accurate Spelling per Minute	Three Most Common Mistakes (Character)
		Level	Time Elapsed	

6a

Pictures 1 to 4 tell a continuous story. The climax of the story in picture 3 is missing. Create the climax for the story and draw it out in the empty box.

6b

Write out the climax you created in 6a in the blanks below.

Eric喜欢吃中餐，可是他用筷子用得不好。他都用叉子和汤匙吃饭。

_____

_____

_____

_____

现在，Eric会用筷子了。他说："面、菜都可以，我都可以用筷子吃。"

7 Practice the strokes to write the characters.

dāo	chā	màn	bǎ	pán
刀	叉	慢	把	盘

吃西餐要用＿＿＿＿ ＿＿＿＿，一口一口＿＿＿＿ ＿＿＿＿吃。
　　　　　　　　　dāo　　chā　　　　　　　　màn　　màn

吃完饭，要＿＿＿碗和＿＿＿子洗一洗。
　　　　　　bǎ　　　　　pán

フ 刀

刀 刀 刀

慢 慢 慢 慢 慢 慢 慢 慢 慢 慢 慢 慢
慢

慢 慢 慢

又 叉 叉

叉 叉 叉

把 把 把 把 把 把 把

把 把 把

盘 盘 盘 盘 盘 盘 盘 盘 盘 盘

盘 盘 盘

8

Refer to the pictures to complete the dialogue below.

: 请问你们要吃中餐还是西餐？

: _____ (Picture 1)

Go 400

In the CD, type the complete dialogue into the section "Exercise> Teacher's Assignment". Print it out and record the time spent on the exercise.

Time Spent: _____

: 请问你要几号餐？

: 我要吃一号餐。

: _____ (Picture 2)

: _____ (Picture 3)

: _____ (Picture 3)

: 我也要喝果汁。

: 我们多了一个人，_____ (Picture 5)

: _____ (Picture 6)

怎么去?
How Do I Go?

1 For each picture, write down its Chinese term and its *pinyin*.

Picture	Chinese	Pinyin
1		
2		
3		
4		
5		
6		
7		

2

Use the helping words and clues provided in each question to complete or form the sentences.

> **A** 飞机　　**B** 地铁　　**C** 出租车　　**D** 公交车
>
> **E** 汽车　　**F** 车站　　**G** 机场　　**H** 火车

① 我上学要先坐地铁，<u>再转火车。</u>　　　　　　　　　（转）

② 坐出租车 <u>比坐公共汽车贵很多。</u>　　　　（比……贵……）

③ <u>我赶 suǒ 以 我 赶得上飞机。</u>　　　　　（赶得上）

④ <u>我比 </u>　　　　　　　　　　　　　　　　（比……慢……）

3

Go to *Exercise > Sentence Quiz* in your **Go 400** to take the quiz. Choose the best two results.

TYPING RECORDS

	Date	Accurate Spelling per Minute	Three Most Common Mistakes (Character)
Record 1			
	Level	Time Elapsed	

	Date	Accurate Spelling per Minute	Three Most Common Mistakes (Character)
Record 2			
	Level	Time Elapsed	

4 Combine the two sentences in each question according to the pictures using the structure "先……再……".

Ⓐ 我要吃早餐。

Ⓑ 我要洗澡。

我先洗澡再吃早餐

Ⓐ 大家要洗手。

Ⓑ 大家要吃饭。

Ⓐ 哥哥要坐公交车。

Ⓑ 哥哥要坐地铁。

哥先坐

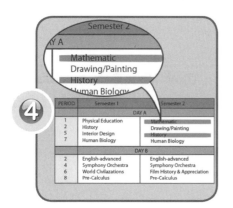

Ⓐ 我要上历史课。

Ⓑ 我要上数学课。

我先上数学课再上历史课

5 Arrange the following sentences in the correct order and write down their corresponding letters in the boxes below.

①

Ⓐ 请问车站在哪里？

Ⓑ 还是找不到车站。

Ⓒ 你要去哪里？

Ⓓ 我找来找去，

➡ (A: | c |)

(B: | | | B |)

②

Ⓐ 你要坐地铁才赶得上飞机。

Ⓑ 坐公交车太慢了，

Ⓒ 坐地铁才快，

Ⓓ 现在坐公交车去机场，

Ⓔ 赶得上八点的飞机吗？

➡ (A: | D | E |)

(B: | B | C | A |)

Go 400

In the CD, type the complete dialogues into the section "Exercise> Teacher's Assignment". Print it out and record the time spent on the exercise.

Time Spent: _____

6 Go to *Exercise > Sentence Quiz* in your **Go 400** to take the quiz. Choose the best two results.

	Date	Accurate Spelling per Minute	Three Most Common Mistakes (Character)
Record 1			
	Level	Time Elapsed	
Record 2	Date	Accurate Spelling per Minute	Three Most Common Mistakes (Character)
	Level	Time Elapsed	

怎么去？   53

7 Jeff (小明) has just returned from a vacation in Hong Kong and Beijing. According to the display below, write down at least six sentences about what Jeff did and how he felt during his vacation. You may also make use of the helping words and sample sentence structures provided.

怎么去?

xiāng gǎng
香港(Hong Kong)

běi jīng
北京(Beijing)

měi guó
美国(the United States)

飞机 / 公交车 / 出租车 / 船

美丽 / 开心 / 听音乐 / 跑步

从……到……

坐……去……

先……再……

去…… (somewhere) (to do something)

比……

我去了北京和香港，我 搭北京。我以为
的
我们假 很们好，目又我 去了演唱会。我
喜又双演唱会。我 先看了美丽风景，再
我 去了我的酒店

8 Practice the strokes to write the characters.

fēi	jī	xiān	cái	gǎn
飞	机	先	才	赶

姐姐要坐＿＿＿ ＿＿＿＿去中国。她要＿＿＿＿坐出租车，
　　　　　　fēi　　　jī　　　　　　　　　xiān

再转地铁去机场＿＿＿ ＿＿＿＿得上。
　　　　　　　cái　　gǎn

乁 飞 飞

飞　飞　飞

机 机 机 机 机 机

机　机　机

先 先 先 先 先 先

先　先　先

才 才 才

才　才　才

赶 赶 赶 赶 赶 赶 赶 赶 赶 赶

赶　赶　赶

我们的大地
The Earth

1 In the table below, write down the *pinyin* and the English translation of each word.

	Chinese	Pinyin	English
1	舒服		
2	干净		
3	脏乱		
4	安全		
5	乱丢		
6	大地		
7	注意		
8	意思		

2 Complete the passage with the words provided.

> **A** 公园 **B** 干净 **C** 脏乱
> **D** 乱丢 **E** 安全 **F** 舒服

我住在公园附近，每天早上都有很多人去公园运动，也有人去那里看花、听小鸟唱歌。

有的人不爱护(cherish)这个公园，在那里＿＿＿＿东西，公园就会很＿＿＿＿。

只要不＿＿＿＿东西，公园就会很＿＿＿＿。只有大家都爱护这个地方(place)，我们才能有一个＿＿＿＿、＿＿＿＿的＿＿＿＿。

3 Go to *Exercise > Sentence Quiz* in your [Go 400] to take the quiz. Choose the best two results.

		Date	Accurate Spelling per Minute	Three Most Common Mistakes (Character)
Record 1				
		Level	Time Elapsed	
		Date	Accurate Spelling per Minute	Three Most Common Mistakes (Character)
Record 2				
		Level	Time Elapsed	

4 Translate the following sentences into Chinese, using either the sentence structure "只有……，才……" or "只要……，就……".

1

The teacher says only the first person to complete the assignment may use the computer.

老师说_____

_____

2

One can only master the Chinese language if he practices it frequently.

学中文_____

_____

3

If you take a taxi, you can make it in time for your flight.

你_____

_____

4

The Earth will only be clean if everybody does not litter.

_____

_____

5 Write a short story according to the pictures provided. Then create your own conclusion and write it out. You may also include an accompanying illustration in the empty box.

① 弟弟打完球回家，_____

_____

② 妈妈_____

_____

③ _____

_____

④ _____

_____

6 Go to *Exercise > Sentence Quiz* in your [Go 400] to take the quiz. Choose the best two results.

		Date	Accurate Spelling per Minute	Three Most Common Mistakes (Character)
Record 1				
	Level		Time Elapsed	
		Date	Accurate Spelling per Minute	Three Most Common Mistakes (Character)
Record 2				
	Level		Time Elapsed	

TYPING RECORDS

7 Practice the strokes to write the characters.

shū	quán	yì	sī	zhù
舒	全	意	思	注

大地健康，大家才能住得____服又安____。
shū quán

这句话的____ ____是要我们____意环保*。
yì si zhù huán bǎo

*环保 environmental protection

舒 舒 舒 舒 舒 舒 舒 舒 舒 舒 舒 舒

舒 舒 舒

全 全 全 全 全 全

全 全 全

意 意 意 意 意 意 意 意 意 意 意 意 意

意 意 意

思 思 思 思 思 思 思 思 思

思 思 思

注 注 注 注 注 注 注 注

注 注 注

Read the following passage and answer the questions below.

qīn ài de
亲爱的*小哥哥：

你为什么不喜欢我了？以前，你会喂我，帮我洗澡，带我去散步。我们一起在草地上跑来跑去，玩游戏；我开心地叫，你开心地笑，每个地方*都有我们的叫声和笑声，我们是最好的朋友。

现在，你很早出去，很晚回来，常常不在家。回到家，你很少说话，不理*爸爸妈妈，也不理我。现在，只有妈妈带我去散步，只有妈妈帮我洗澡，只有妈妈照顾我。我想知道你为什么不开心？为什么不喜欢我了？

你爱的狗狗上

*亲爱的 dear　　*地方 place　　*理 respond to someone

1 Which of the following sentences reflect the content of the passage accurately?

☐ 现在是妈妈在照顾小狗。

☐ 小哥哥不照顾小狗，因为他和爸妈吵架了。

☐ 小狗不喜欢小哥哥了。

2 According to the passage, what did "小哥哥" used to do for his dog?

_____

_____

3 If you were the recipient of this letter, how would you respond? Write down at least two sentences of your response below.

_____

_____

工作天地
Work and Occupations

1 Write down the occupation in each picture in Chinese and its *pinyin*.

①

Chinese

Pinyin

②

Chinese

Pinyin

③

Chinese

Pinyin

④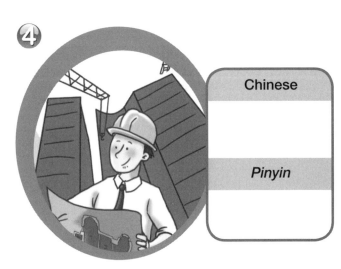

Chinese

Pinyin

⑤

Chinese

Pinyin

⑥

Chinese

Pinyin

2 Rewrite the following sentences so that the person becomes the subject at the beginning of each sentence.

① 律师是哥哥最有兴趣的职业。

哥哥最有兴趣的职业是(　　　　)。

② 旅行是爷爷最喜欢的活动。

_____

③ 周末上班的工作，他不要。

_____

④ 清理地上的脏东西是我常常做的事。

_____

3 Go to *Exercise > Sentence Quiz* in your [Go 400] to take the quiz. Choose the best two results.

TYPING RECORDS		Date	Accurate Spelling per Minute	Three Most Common Mistakes (Character)
	Record **1**			
		Level	Time Elapsed	
	Record **2**	Date	Accurate Spelling per Minute	Three Most Common Mistakes (Character)
		Level	Time Elapsed	

4 Match a phrase in the left column to another phrase in the right column and connect them with "需要" to form a coherent sentence.

A 学中文	**a** 天天练习
B 运动员	**b** 多听、多说
C 演员	**c** 对电视、电影有兴趣
D 律师和警员	**d** 筷子或汤匙
E 生病	**e** 多休息
F 吃中餐	

① 运动员需要天天练习，才能得到好成绩。

② _____

③ _____

④ _____

⑤ _____

5 Go to *Exercise > Sentence Quiz* in your ⊙ Go400 to take the quiz. Choose the best two results.

TYPING RECORDS		Date	Accurate Spelling per Minute	Three Most Common Mistakes (Character)
	Record 1			
		Level	Time Elapsed	
	Record 2	Date	Accurate Spelling per Minute	Three Most Common Mistakes (Character)
		Level	Time Elapsed	

6a Look at the picture and fill in the blanks accordingly.

我的姐姐是＿＿＿＿＿＿，她的工作是＿＿＿＿＿＿，参加比赛。她每天要从＿＿＿＿＿一直练习到＿＿＿＿＿，有时＿＿＿＿＿也要练习。姐姐说，她每天都要练习很久，可是她很喜欢打球，只要有＿＿＿＿＿就不累。

6b Model after the examples in 6a and below and write a paragraph describing a relative's or a friend's occupation.

我的爸爸是工人，他的工作是帮别
gài fáng zi
人盖房子*。他每天七点就去上班，一直到下午六点才回家。爸爸的工作很辛苦，可是他还是每天认真地上班。

*盖房子 build a house

_____

_____

_____

_____

_____

7 Practice the strokes to write the characters.

diàn	huò	xìng	qù	zhí
店	或	兴	趣	直

表哥对做＿＿＿员＿＿＿做厨师都有＿＿＿＿＿＿，
　　　　diàn　　 huò　　　　　　　　xìng　　 qù

他一＿＿＿在做这两种工作。
　　 zhí

店店店店店店店店
店	店	店			

或或或或或或或
或	或	或			

兴兴兴兴兴兴
兴	兴	兴			

趣趣趣趣趣趣趣趣趣趣趣趣趣
趣趣
趣	趣	趣			

直直直直直直直直
直	直	直			

8 In the following passage, Sophia Green describes her father, mother, and older brother's weekly schedule. Read it carefully before answering the questions that follow.

> 我爸爸是医师，他星期二要从上午一直工作到晚上。可是，爸爸星期三早上不用帮病人看病，他可以送我去上学。
>
> 我妈妈是律师，每天从早上九点到下午五点上班。除了做律师，她每个星期还要去中文学校教两次中文，每次教一个半小时。
>
> 我哥哥从星期一到星期五都要上课，星期三晚上和星期六要打工，他是一个店员。
>
> 除了星期二和星期三，我们每天都一起吃晚餐。星期天我们全家常常一起去打球，可是这个星期天不行。
>
> 爸爸、妈妈和哥哥上班都很忙，可是他们都很喜欢他们的工作。

GO Chinese School
Remedial Class Notice

Teacher: **Mrs. Green**
Date of Class: **23rd May (Sunday)**
Time of Class: **9:30~11a.m.**

1

Which of the following weekly schedules belong to Sophia's father, mother, and older brother? Label them with the correct terms of address ("爸爸", "妈妈", and "哥哥"). The gray areas indicate work or school, while the triangular symbol indicates an important task for the day.

A [ ]

	日	一	二	三	四	五	六
上午			■		■	■	■
下午		■	■		■		
晚上			■	■			

B [ ]

	日	一	二	三	四	五	六
上午		■	■	■	■	■	■
下午		■	■	■			
晚上							

C [ ]

	日	一	二	三	四	五	六
上午	▲	■	■	■	■	■	
下午		■	■	■	■	■	
晚上				■			

D [ ]

	日	一	二	三	四	五	六
上午		■	■		■	■	▲
下午		■	■	■	■	■	
晚上				■			

2

Check the box next to the sentence that reflects the content of the passage accurately.

A [ ] 哥哥每天放学回家时，爸爸都在医院上班。

B [ ] 星期二不能全家一起吃饭，因为爸爸要上班。

C [ ] 星期六上午或下午，都有人能带Sophia出去玩。

D [ ] 星期三上午爸爸和妈妈都不用上班。

E [ ] 这个星期天上午，妈妈需要去上班。

REVIEW 2

1 Fill in the boxes with the words provided, according to each row's category. Write down the *pinyin* of all the words.

> **A** 律师　　**B** 打电话　　**C** 地铁　　**D** 盘子
> **E** 脏乱　　**F** 西餐　　**G** 转车　　**H** 客厅　　**I** 本

① | shuì fáng
睡房 | 厨房 | 书房 | |

② | | 洗澡 | 睡觉 | 吃饭 | |

③ | | 汤匙 | 筷子 | 碗 | |

④ | | 条 | 支 | 只 | |

⑤ | | 飞机 | 出租车 | 火车 | |

⑥ | | 演员 | 运动员 | 店员 | |

⑦ | | 乾净 | 舒服 | 安静 | |

2

Describe the items in each picture by using the structure "numeral + measure word + noun".

桌上有＿＿＿＿＿＿＿＿＿＿＿

＿＿＿＿＿＿＿＿＿＿＿＿＿＿

＿＿＿＿＿＿＿＿＿＿＿＿＿＿

＿＿＿＿＿＿＿＿＿＿＿＿＿＿

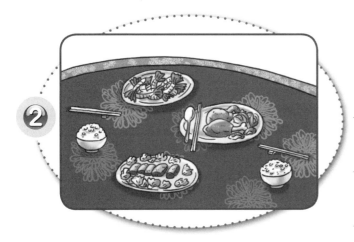

桌上有＿＿＿＿＿＿＿＿＿＿＿

＿＿＿＿＿＿＿＿＿＿＿＿＿＿

＿＿＿＿＿＿＿＿＿＿＿＿＿＿

＿＿＿＿＿＿＿＿＿＿＿＿＿＿

我养了＿＿＿＿＿＿＿＿＿＿＿

＿＿＿＿＿＿＿＿＿＿＿＿＿＿

＿＿＿＿＿＿＿＿＿＿＿＿＿＿

＿＿＿＿＿＿＿＿＿＿＿＿＿＿

3 Use the following information to answer the questions below. You may answer Question 2 in English.

① 小明坐什么时候的飞机？

_____

② 他要从_____飞到_____。

③ 飞机要飞十四个小时才会到北京，小明什么时候会到北京？

_____

④ 去机场，坐出租车最快也最_____；坐_____最便宜，坐_____比坐_____便宜二十五块。

⑤ 坐火车和坐公交车到机场都要_____。

⑥ 小明要上飞机得怎么走？

_____

_____

（先……再……）

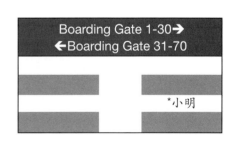

4

Write a description of Older Sister's job. For every picture, form one or more sentences using the sentence structure as specified in the question. You may also use the helping words provided in the box below.

> **A** 辛苦   **B** 晚上   **C** 白天   **D** 工作   **E** 安全
>
> **F** 乾净   **G** 办公室   **H** guó jiā gōng yuán 国家公园 (National Park)   **I** 喜欢

①

我的姐姐_____

_____

（是……）

②

_____

_____

（除了……，还……）

③

_____

_____

（有时……，有时……）

④

_____

_____

（只要……，就……）

5 Read the following conversation between Jeff ("J") and Michael ("M") carefully. Imagine you are Michael. Use the information in the dialogue to write a letter to 小贵, inviting him to join you on a vacation. Your letter should include your travel dates, your destination, as well as the destination attractions.

J： 新年假期你要去哪里？

M： 我想在家休息，在家里看电视节目或用电脑。

J： 放假别一直在家，我们去旅行好吗？

M： 你要去哪里旅行？太热的地方，我不想去。

J： 我们一起去日本(Japan)或香港(Hong Kong)，好不好？
<small>rì běn</small> <small>xiāng gǎng</small>

M： 日本我去过了，我不想去。去香港可以做什么？

J： 我们可以买便宜的衣服、鞋子，还可以吃好吃的中餐。电视节目说，晚上的香港比白天更美丽。晚上我们可以找一家餐厅，一边吃饭，一边看最美丽的香港。

M： 我想要去香港看一看。我们要怎么去？

J： 我们可以坐飞机去。从这里到香港，一天有三班飞机，很方便。

M： 到了香港，我们要住哪里？

J： 我姑姑住在那里，她的家有客房。我们可以一起住我姑姑家。我姑姑还说住她家，不用钱！

M： 太好了！我可以找别人一起去吗？

J： 好，可是不要找你的弟弟或妹妹，他们太小了。

M： 我想找小贵一起去。

J： 好。

_____ :

_____

_____

_____

_____

_____

_____

_____

_____

_____

(date)

6 Read Kevin, Michael, and Pauline's descriptions of their home and label the following floor plans accordingly with their names.

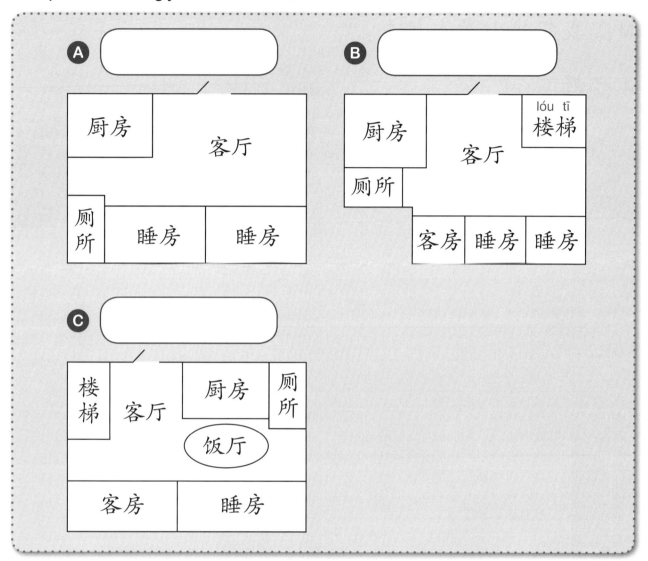

Kevin : 我家和Pauline家一样，有两间睡房。

我的睡房在厕所旁边。

Michael：我家的厨房在客厅左边，睡房在客房右边。

我家二楼还有一间书房和一间睡房。

Pauline：一进到我家，就会看到客厅。

我家的睡房，一间在楼上，一间在楼下。